Lost Letters and Windfalls

Rustin Larson

San Francisco | Fairfield | Delhi

Lost Letters and Windfalls
Rustin Larson

Copyright ©2020 by Rustin Larson

First Edition.

ISBN: 978-1-4218-3672-0

Library of Congress Control Number: 2020944537

Cover art: "Lost Letters" by Rustin Larson. Mixed media.

All rights reserved. Printed in the United States of America. No part of this book may be used or reproduced in any manner whatsoever without written permission except in the case of brief quotations embodied in critical articles and reviews. For information contact:

1ST WORLD LIBRARY
PO Box 2211
Fairfield, Iowa 52556
www.1stworldpublishing.com

BLUE LIGHT PRESS
www.bluelightpress.com
Email: bluelightpress@aol.com

PRAISE FOR *LOST LETTERS AND WINDFALLS*

"Among cornfields, junkyards, and a Dairy Queen, the eclectic cast of Rustin Larson's *Lost Letters and Windfalls* marches across a rural stage: an old woman small 'like a burlap bag/ full of nylons,' family members, angels, finches, the wind, the muse, and a young girl in a Degas painting. The poet asserts: 'The light falls upon all things. I have/ my memory of you—quiet as a/ picture frame among all these broken houses.' In poem after poem, Larson captures images firmly cast in time yet eternal—even slightly holy: 'But here's what we are: each man, each woman,/ each neuter object, a church.'"

"'Listen,' Larson urges, 'the world/ begins in a moment.' The moments described in these poems are painterly and vivid. The poet trusts only his 'sense of touch.' They conjure a world of isolated stillness where characters can 'choose to stand outside of ourselves if we wish, the snow falling.' But also a world of connection where 'planets are fishing/ for us, wanting/ us' and '[t]he moon is the friend of the earth / and the earth of the sun.' This is a book of small tendernesses and lightning bolts that will stay with you."

Nynke Passi, Director, MFA in Creative Writing, MIU

"He makes everything greater because he's a smart singer, every poem is a win. Moments shine with an unselfconscious voice. We cannot imagine how easily paint can be applied if we just speak in real time of consequential things with a depth of heart. Within that modest framework the passage of words has a capability and a sphere of influence without limits. The poetry dynamics here are a genuine voice, believable encounters, and the ability to make everything new with the belief that no one's watching you, and nothing can come of it, and there's nothing to get. This is poetry at its best."

Grace Cavalieri, Review of *Library Rain* in The Washington Independent Review of Books

"Like a painter saturating the colors of Earth, exalting its geography from delirious beauty to war nightmares, Larson takes the reader on a dreamlike journey, filled with flashbacks, family memories, and ghosts."

Helene Cardona, Review of *The Philosopher Savant* in The Enchanting Verses Literary Review

"Even for Rustin Larson, a master of invention, *Lost Letters and Windfalls* breaks into new territory. I love the images he chooses and how he transforms them. It's fascinating to see where he goes in the shorter jewel-like poems of this book. Brilliant writing, a delight on every page, a joy to read!"

Diane Frank, Author of *While Listening to the Enigma Variations: New and Selected Poems*

"Rustin Larson is a terrific, elegant, original poet whose voice rings so truly we become better people just by reading him."

Naomi Shihab Nye

Acknowledgements

These poems made their first appearances in the following journals; the author thanks the editors for their efforts and kindnesses:

Black Buzzard Review: "Window Light"
Boundary 2: "Having Arrived in Washington, D.C., I Seek Employment," "Leaning into the Mirror I Address My Image"
California Quarterly: "The Outer Air," "Those Two are Indeed the Same Man," "Degas," "Rust," "Attending Sleep," "Fox Grape," "Ghost Breath"
G.W. Review: "To the Muse," "Tornado Watch," "The World Begins in a Moment"
The Issue: "Denouement"
Loonfeather: "Twilight Accompanied by Flute," "Caretaker"
Lyrical Iowa: "Entering the Mood of the Day," "Woman with Parasol Turned to the Left," "Trumpet Vine," "Geodesic"
The MacGuffin: "You Read Aloud"
The Mid-America Poetry Review: "Abandoned Farm," "Living in Iowa," "Pigs"
Panoply: "Both Halves Together," "Elegy in a Cornfield," "Floating Hearts"
Phantasmagoria: "It Could Be Worse," "Strange Courage," "Release"
Poem: "Windfalls"
Poetry East: "I Could Say Now"

"Both Halves Together" also appeared in *The Wine-Dark House* (Blue Light Press, 2009).

Content

Rust 3

Windfalls 4

Entering the Mood of the Day 6

It Could Be Worse 7

Strange Courage 8

Release 9

Both Halves Together 10

Elegy in a Cornfield 11

A Quick Tour of Europe 12

Ghost Breath 13

Fox Grape 14

Attending Sleep 15

Trumpet Vine 16

Degas 17

Woman with Parasol Turned to the Left 18

Spanish Music 19

Those Two are Indeed the Same Man 20

Floating Hearts 22

The Outer Air 23

Twilight Accompanied by Flute 24

October 25

First Snow 26

Shimek Forest after Ice Storm 27

Night Music 28

Caretaker 29

Living in Iowa 30

Abandoned Farm ... 31
Travel ... 32
Are We There Yet? ... 33
Window Light ... 34
Pigs ... 35
To the Muse ... 37
Tornado Watch ... 38
The World Begins in a Moment ... 39
I Could Say Now ... 41
Having Arrived in Washington, D.C., I Seek Employment ... 42
Leaning into a Mirror I Address My Image ... 44
You Read Aloud ... 46
Lightning ... 48
Denouement ... 49
Lost ... 50
For You ... 51
Geodesic ... 52
Cedar River ... 53

About the Author ... 54

for Caroline

Lost Letters and Windfalls

Rust

There was a junkyard I loved.
It lived a thousand miles
into the trees. We found a tire
we could patch for the jalopy.
We would get some Dairy Queen
on the way home. I was a lucky
dog. I saw great mountains
burning. Sitting Bull spoke to us
over the radio. Blue steel clouds
came from the north and hailed
pearls of ice in summer, the air
ripped by lightning. The weird
would weight the branches.
It didn't even know it had a name.
It fluffed out its feathers.
Its breast was the color of rust.

WINDFALLS

Old woman stooping for windfall pears: her lawn
where Highway 92
crosses Route 57.
She is small, like a burlap bag
full of nylons.
Her house, a mystery
of knocking winds. The few seconds

I watch her as I pass—
she bends
for a pear, placing it softly
in a metal bucket—stick
like a stamp in the corner
of my brain; I think

of the bare tree
stretching over my childhood,
melting into a stooped old woman
reaching for something she'd lost. "My
heart!" The yellow
torso has a red bruise; she groans holding the fruit
like sun breaking folds
of grey.

From the corner
of my eye, throbbing
in the rearview mirror: my winking pulse. I let it
pass.

Mother carves fruit with a little knife.
Mother, it's gone forever.

Entering the Mood of the Day

It's like
pushing angels
off a bridge.

Zodiac clock.
Mechanical bears.
Floating city.

Italian woman
says, "no unnerstand"
and then dies.

That's sad.
I can't change that.
But it's Easter.

It Could Be Worse

This train wreck
of a conscience,

this blitzkrieg
of snow and ice,

this tsunami
of bad memories,

this desert
of misunderstanding,

this year
of contaminated
minutes.

Strange Courage

New leaves
have risen
from the shamrock
again,

opening
in morning,
growing near
the sounds

of the window
when the wasp
hangs its nest
in the eaves,

or when the wren
taps madly
on the window-
pane.

Release

There is a joy
this late hour
reserved

for those who
having reached
extreme age

give up
worry
and breathe

the inhuman air.

Both Halves Together

Like the man who says, "It's my invention;
it came to me while I was on the john!"
I know exactly what to do with my life:

one half will repair the spines of dwarfs,
so they will stand corrected; the other half
will get to know our feathered friends better

like a bitter colony of lice, will sit
in golden kinship as autumn smoke rises
from the leaves, will chew on a piece of

celery and feel how good its stringy wateriness
tastes in the open air. Both halves together
will wish they had gotten into real estate

early on, but mostly they will admire
those who spent their lives serving humanity,
those who rescued children from the jaws of mice,

those who poisoned the silver-skinned men
from Pluto with orange juice, those who are
tucked away in the ground with a few

roses on top of them, and a few sweet words
cut into the sadness.

Elegy in a Cornfield

Your fangs, Mozart, how ticklish
they made my ankles feel as you burst
from a mound of dirty socks
bounding, King Leo in your African inscape,
over the slick maple floor of my bedroom,
your tiny claws clattering delicate scrimshaw
on the varnish, making mother scream
in her pigeony flutter, as the wind blew
from the window blowing nests of fur
from your favorite perch
like ghosts in the light twisting with spores. Anyway,
we buried you in this cornfield.

A Quick Tour of Europe

old fortress:
charcoal on stone

casino
of stale bread cubes,
little fairy house,
chocolate ice cream

Mozart's harpsichord,
jeweled tomb
of an emperor

Beethoven's October:
bright orange finches shivering
on an apple tree

Ghost Breath

A Chinese woman
flips through
a Chinese newspaper
and clutches
her pocket book.
Ghost money.

She zips her coat up
for the cold.
Ghost breath. Vapor.

What does it
mean
when she walks away
with her handbag
strapped over
her right shoulder?

Why does it
look like she is counting
the fingers
of her gloves?

Fox Grape

Fox grape is killing the bush in our side yard,
So Caroline and I take part of the afternoon
To kill the fox grape.
This is herbal warfare started, I think,
By the weed who invaded at the base
Of the shrubbery and climbed
To daylight, choking every branch
It touched. *A bit like the thorns
Guarding Sleeping Beauty*, Caroline
Says as we hack our way, yanking
And pulling vine. On the sub-atomic
Level, these are insubstantial mists,
And beyond that these vines are nothing.
Mere thoughts, if that; yet they cut my hands.

Attending Sleep

Sitting, waiting for a play to begin,
I see you take your seat
Ten rows down from me.
Nothing can cure this.
Where one sprig is cut,
Another grows.
I dream of your face, then wake.
The moon slides silently
All night long above me.

Trumpet Vine

10:05 rolls through, creates a temporary
barrier across 4th. She stands on her threshold
smoking, watching. It's dark. The crickets chirp
a half-hearted lullaby to the train's fading noise.

Two dogs, Chihuahuas,
yip at a stranger passing on the sidewalk.
The street lamps perform their fluttering indecision.
Hemingway had a penchant for describing booze

as crisp and cool and clean on the tongue.
She has read a lot lately, pre-formed
thoughts to fill a sleepless night. A new train,
from the west now. How perfect. The darkness

protects her house. She cannot
see the rails, but feels they're there.
She has nothing to lean on but the ladder
of trumpet vine bracing the porch. Dying

is a long project for some people. The hills
she can't see are out there, maybe. Hemingway
goes on in the next chapter—it's getting close
to Independence Day—a projectile of fire arches above.

Degas

A young girl
measures
the width

of her shoulders,
washes
with a clean sponge

from a shallow
pan
of water.

A young woman
enters
with the dampness

of violets
around
her eyes.

Woman With Parasol Turned to the Left

We in hushed cool rooms of afterlife
can sometimes recall the breath of July
rankling a passage through sage, loosestrife,
and sometimes recall an aqua parasol
against such chiseled and determined clouds,
the rustled hush of a white summer dress,
the sea's aerosol and echoed canopy
of chill blue, the stirring crickets
of the grass, the kernels of wild wheat
polished by the sun's bright acetylene.

Spanish Music

My private tree
full of angels,
study

of floral
arrangements,
violet walls,
malleable faces.

White tool shed
bordered by red
brick, marigolds;

cottonwoods
alternating
white to green,
day to day

collecting
harmonies,
never easy.

Spanish music
played
too fast,

even
by
Spaniards.

Those Two are Indeed the Same Man

Walking back to their attic
after an all night drunk, there's
the baker's window, lacerations

of an electric bulb through cracks
of a pulled blind. They sigh,
wonder how the modern age will live.

I would rather be a sponge,
says the blond one. The brown-haired nods
knowing they are both sponges.

It's all right this companionship hazed
and warmed by booze. They could have been
brothers all their lives and not known.

The blond lights a cigarette and touches
the arm of his friend. They both point
to the clock tower. Too drunk

to tell time. If it were daylight, they'd go
to the cafe and watch old men play chess.
The world is not dead. If they'd knock

on a door, someone would shoot them.
This is what we get for living
in such a small town, says the blond one.

We should have moved to Pittsburgh, says the other.
Then they stand saying nothing, entranced
how the other's face changes. Women. No. Not women.

I think we're dead, says the brown-haired one.
No, says the other. Yes.
Yes, I think we are finally dead.

Floating Hearts

'Sterling silver chain, free floating heart.'
A thin-armed man swings charms for girls:
their hair chopped black. His olive fingers
pinch the chain on a single link; the cinnabar
heart veined with cloud-white blood, immune
to joy or pain, just one dollar complete.
Perhaps it's reiteration
to chain a heart around one's neck,
but its chill there, to touch and twist
and push to one's lips is a satisfaction
beyond desire. The two girls pay their fee;
the olive hands hold a mirror entranced
by their floating hearts.

THE OUTER AIR

The tree limb
alone
is burning

from the core,
the fire-blood
has risen

Near this red
pool
we'll rest

and feed
the day
more ashes

Twilight Accompanied by Flute

The steep ladder of thirtysecond notes
reaches twilight, quickly dissolves to breath.
Stand and watch the dry moon float
to absorb the body's emptiness.

Stand in a doorless doorway and turn
memory to sand: the ruined mill's walls
leeched with ivy; inside the pit churns:
black leaves battered by little waterfalls.

And inside, the trail pulses in moon.
The air is blue and silky and rushed.
Reaching for a branch of dogwood,
the petals drop: stars, fevered and hushed.

A brittle stairway of thirtysecond notes
touches twilight, becomes breath, floats.

October

The orange day draws up
birds like evaporating
water – blue winged
with an open sound:
spaces between
leaves, trees growing
rich in emptiness.

First Snow

The flurries
begin
to whiten
the strip

of grass,
our lack
of speech,

the crows
in
the air.

Shimek Forest After Ice Storm

Some trees bent, sickly
gleaming as dreams in glass;

others bowed in prayers so deep
the entire woodland, crystal,

chimes fragilely; I can hear
the obsidian inside the ice and know

what makes them deep.
Now a blue jay glides through the glass

of the city of skeletons:
the streets, sparkling, tapestry threaded

by dew, by freezing rain.

Night Music

The blindest among us pulls out a harmonica,
passes it around the campfire. Wings,
branches, leaves raised like braille
in the chrome casing. Shimmerings
of evaporating music, notes flooding
the blackness: each warbles his vision: meadowlark,
song uncorked. Reddened by campfire,
we are strangers. Yet each song pools around the flame.

Caretaker

It's snowing, micro lace, crystalized roses,
and it's the souls of all the dead.
Stone: a bony head;
fallen branches: a road littered with whitened bones;
on a rise a granite soldier poses
above a yellow sign: NO PASSING ZONE.
And it's snowing and the flakes pile up.

Jim Swimmer died in an oxygen tent.
He could finger "Red Wing" on guitar
like a railroad bum bent
on resuscitating the ghost of Woody Guthrie
with a cigarette and a lonesome train harpoon.
Swimmer, it snows like a prayer for you.

And all I've to do is fill this cup
and strain a glance into the skies
to be awakened. The souls of heaven
flutter down and cool my eyes.

Living in Iowa

pools of wind

shadows
on the periphery

goldenrod ditches
yellow dust
snow

late november
clouds

gravel road
web of trees

squirrels
cracking
grey light

graveyard

the skull
of a cow

Abandoned Farm

Sometimes, November, the sun
floods ruby over fields in stubble,
the last jewels caught
on some broken window's rubble.
Six dark geese fly
over exhausted runs of Queen Anne's lace
into the evening's first weeping star.

Travel

cloudless river
peeling white sheds

industrial clouds
private sin

truck driver's cab
fills with light

Are We There Yet?

Mother checks
her compact,
sprays her bourbon hair.

Father see the billboard
for country ham,
hangs his thick hands

on the steering wheel,
rolls his toothpick
from one corner

of his mouth
to
the other.

Window Light

You switch the vent so cold air can knife through,
in Iowa, the fragrance thick, wet,
the farmland harvested, stalks broken, strewn
on ruts, the moonlight white as medicine.

Some houses near the highway: windows,
jack-o-lantern eyes.
On a La-Z-Boy a bald man reclines, smokes,
props up his naked feet and reads his white

newspaper. We drive: headlights extend like arms
of the blind. Soon, a machine shed: men
wrench spark plugs off an engine: oil smudged arms
glisten, fluorescent tubes blast white on them.

And then, ahead, in a burning yellow window,
beside her bed a girl slides from her clothes.

Pigs

The man carves the snarl of a lion
from a trunk of red cedar

with the knife he can throw so easily and swiftly.
In the background

a baby cries like a wounded pecari, and the man's wife
emerges from the shadowy room; she is stirring

yellow cornmeal batter in a blue bowl. No tengo
el queso de la luna! The man screams.

Mantequilla de la mariposa! He slaps the bowl
from her hands. Then her tears like little candle flames.

A mesquite fire crackles in the burning place
and the tortillas scorch bronze with the face of Jesus

in their sacred ovals. The man lifts
his baby in his scarred red hands and squeezes out

"Ah, my fat one, what an artist
I would have been had I not been thrown

in the company of pigs." Gunfire
bleeds the air outside. And in his mind

the man sees the sun sinking into the smoke
and fiery sweat of a roasting boar.

Let the fiesta live before all the death.
Let the teeth glisten with the grease of the pigs.

To the Muse

When I think about the holy occupations
I carpe diem myself into submission.
The wall is myself and my ear
hears the empty spaces that have
made up this planet. I feel cured
in short. Knowing the right way to face
the wind, I walk into it, it doesn't
bother me. There are certain terms
we have settled on—it knows it's
the same wind as Jamestown or
Plymouth. I have had my feasts there
and I continue to take them with
me in this brown paper bag.
Instead of contradictions
it contains the resolutions in its
emptiness. A violent emptiness is
the wind, and it can pick up whole
houses, if it wants, piling them like
crumpled egg shells in an open field.
The light falls upon all things. I have
my memory of you—quiet as a
picture frame among all these broken houses.

Tornado Watch

The old house is crumbling from sympathy.
I'm afraid to go down the basement;
there a dim red light is burning,
a little S-shaped man hunched over the sink
developing black-and-white portraits.

I look outside at the yellow stillness.
Unnatural green leaves hold their glowing
photographic poise, drop no rain water.
Summers group around me, smiling folk saying:
"It almost seems you belong here."

The fossil trilobites stare in black
pin-beams from a magnified display.
The electric lamp haloes long silences.

Crouched under the bench, I hold my head
by my knees
and remember two photographs of myself.

The World Begins in a Moment

This is easy as saying November
begins, or my love for you (which has never

ended) has begun. I feel unecclesiastic.
I talk in soft whispers, as to never

disturb the dead leaves—their pattern final
like father, pater. Patter was once a word

to describe them as they fell. But no more.
They whisper as I do. A crowd of monks

walks across the hill's ridge. I'm seated
at morning's late beginning, the sun near

its winter angle. Ten-twenty on Monday,
no one enters the chapel. If I said

cathedral it would be clear. Universal.
But here's what we are: each man, each woman,

each neuter object, a church. We can choose
to stand outside ourselves if we wish, the snow falling,

carols spreading rose and yellow from windows.
Sometimes I wonder—where do I begin?

I see a woman bury her lover
under blankets of dry autumn leaves. Their

laughter continuing. And you too bury me
with a warm leaf fall. You

and me, not exactly sharing dreams, but
consenting to dance, softly, the music

slowly changing to trees. I, for my moods, can only
trust my sense of touch. Listen. The world

begins in a moment. I'll keep you posted,
my unrequited fiction.

I Could Say Now

I want you
or I must have you
but you would

leave your coat on
as before
and hold me

at arm's length
to prove
how much older

you were,
and I would pick
up your hand

and notice
your bones
light

and fragile
as
a sparrow's.

Having Arrived in Washington, D.C., I Seek Employment

Bus stop: a young woman anoints
her coffee colored palms with moist

lotion. On her lap a bible is split open. She eyes
it and rubs her hands. Dogwood trees white

petals brush over the stop's transparent canopy.
On my lap, like one good ocean wave, my poetry

in large green cover curves.
The white spring light observes

my room as I left it: the bed,
unmade, splashing onto the floor's hard wood,

the venus fly trap, the books—the few—
Greek lyrics, Williams, Faulkner, and Thoreau.

My books, uncomfortable now
that I'm away from them... I know

the kitchen shelf they're on must seem
like a hospital ward in a patient's drugged dream:

white, bare, but for consciousness
and the clean scent

of white petals drifting, tapping
against dim glass, as the day swirls trapping

grass blades beneath serpent paths of wind.
But how shall I rescind

this promise I've made to myself? Work
must be found, yet I must find places to work

my words. Two buses come now in couplet lines,
pull up to the stop, end to end, and rhyme.

Leaning Into a Mirror I Address My Image

What is more satisfying than leaning
on one's hands as they try to push
a building down? What is better,

to learn in school, or to learn
from example? Lao Tsu said the king
who is loved best is the one the people

hardly know is there. With no
examples, it is a lesson
kings hardly follow. That is why

we the people are so wretched.
That is why we push buildings
down with our bare hands. That is

why we are destined to such short lives.
But wait. Are we really any worse off
than our friends who lived in caves?

Has our perception of the "good" changed any
in the past million years? Do we still
have to put up with our spouses' snoring?

These are questions to answer yes and no by.
It's not that you hear or understand the question—
the important thing is the answer. That is why

you were given that small electricity coursing
up and down your spine. That is why
your fingers find their way into the wrong

fire and get burned by believing in the good
too hard. And that is why when I tell you to sit,
you sit, and you look up at me

with those soft brown eyes, and wag your tail,
and hope like hell I don't leave town
and vanish from your life.

You Read Aloud

1985. I see our daughter, little beacon
pulse on the sonogram. You lie on a table.
She is in this square glass "paragraph,"
a story so lucid it seems a friend.
Outside, brown leaves and an engine
rasp. The driving. Miles and miles.

Back home though, you smile.
When the kitchen clock shines, it's a beacon
of quiet time. I touch the petal of an ingenuous
violet. The petal falls to the table.
You slice open a letter from a friend
while I read a newspaper paragraph

which shows, with a pair of graphs,
how, thousands of miles
away, missiles point at us. Our reporter "friend"
suggests we'd have little warning. Some beacon
would detect the first launch. Then on a table
in some war room we'd be a black X for the engines

of war. Start the car's engine.
Where would we go? A paragraph
into the letter, you pat your hand on the table
then reach for your tea. Meaningless miles.
You read the letter aloud: a beacon
crowns a water tower in the Midwest. A friend

from childhood is still a friend.
He and I would play cowboys and injuns,
and later Hiroshima, bombing a balsa wood town with the beacon
flash of a cherry bomb. Paragraphs
from history couldn't make the miles
seem any closer. Now I'm here, at a table

with you, half the table
of contents of me. Our small friend
swims in your womb. You smile.
A jet engine
rattles our apartment. One final paragraph:
"Don't give up," says the friend. That beacon.

Lightning

In the grey sky garden,
lightning flowers.

The crocuses lie
asleep
under black soil.

The spearmint rises
though cold.

Through a pale
handful
of aster seed

my wish begins
to touch the rainfall.

The blind asters
touch
the lightning's voice.

Denouement

There could be worse things than to die in your sleep or in a haze of morphine. Outside woods growing in a deep ravine: aspen chestnut buckeye poison ivy oak. The air system shushes the summer noise of the nearby turnpike. Cold. The house of death.

The last time you were rational you shook my hand and stared at me as if we just met. I am the stranger who married the daughter who hid ganja in her knitting bag. Our children's photos are turned frame down on the basketball mute television. You seem to approve of, instead, the litter of grandchildren from the lawyer son who's just flown in from North Carolina. Their pictures are upright and can see you

as you sleep long now, curled like an infant, your hair downy, your breath gentle into whatever noise snows over your blanketed body. Under the lamp, your wife knits for the glow and waits, and your children sit in your room and speak softly to the afternoon.

Lost

And you.
Something is swimming
beneath the ice.

We want the grey old
winter to climb down
through the smoking pines.

Fire stoked high
with dry twigs,
the planets fishing

for us, wanting
us.

For You

I swear, friendship hangs on the hardest
wind.
The moon is the friend of the earth

and the earth of the sun.
Strangers are not present. A wind

who loves to play in her invisible
garden is near.

We won't trouble her flowers,
believe me.

Geodesic

I'm going to find those phosphorescent blue veins of rock and lie on them until I hear the oceans empty. I'm going to wield that tough wire inside my head and hook it onto a crater in the moon and hope the dust never moves from its place. Moonlight is always borrowed light from the sun—that's what they tell you—but never mind them; I happen to know the person who translates all the letters that come from the moon, and he says we've never seen the bright side.

I may just bunch cabbages for a living, or sign my name to worthless documents. Or maybe none of that. I've seen tear-moss grow so early in the spring and yellow dew spiders scatter, in all their family ramifications, to the soft tongue hollows of fallen trees. I may go there... if I follow the right direction. What is it they call the path the arrow flies?

Cedar River

As I walked to my room one night with all this longing and love running through me like two unmixable rivers, I thought of how hawk feathers sometimes rain from the branches that hang over the Cedar River. And they spin down instantly with no speed or smell and lip the water with clean light affection and then glide like barges, sideways, bobbing to the dimples and snarls in the brown season-fostering current.

And when all objects have floated to the dam, I wait for the sound the river has to bring me. It comes curling like a golden wave—it happens to be the sound that hollowed the mud banks and exposed all the roots so they stream out of the river wall like so many tangled thoughts or incommunicable wires ripped from their cabled divisions. It is a curling sound that comes, like the bending of branches, and those flutes that are constructed for such an intangible length of time offer their fluttering from the neck of trees—where one limb becomes the next and then strikes the clouds with its own lightning bolt.

About the Author

Rustin Larson's poetry has appeared in The New Yorker, The Iowa Review, and North American Review. He won 1st Editor's Prize from Rhino and was a prize winner in The National Poet Hunt and The Chester H. Jones Foundation contests. A graduate of the Vermont College MFA in Writing, Larson was an Iowa Poet at The Des Moines National Poetry Festival, and a featured poet at the Poetry at Round Top Festival.

He is a poetry professor at Maharishi University, a writing instructor at Kirkwood Community College, and has also been a writing instructor at Indian Hills Community College.

His honors and awards also include Pushcart Prize Nominee (seven times, 1988-2010); featured writer, DMACC Celebration of the Literary Arts, 2007, 2008; and finalist, New England Review Narrative Poetry Competition, 1985.

Books by Rustin Larson

The Philosopher Savant Crosses the River (New Chicago, 2019.)
Library Rain (Conestoga Zen Press, 2018.)
Howling Enigma (Conestoga Zen Press, 2018.)
Pavement (Blue Light Press, 2017.)
The Philosopher Savant (Glass Lyre Press, 2015.)
Bum Cantos, Winter Jazz, & The Collected Discography of Morning (Blue Light Press, 2013.)
Waiting for Evening to Come (Conestoga Zen Press, 2012.)
The Wine-Dark House (Blue Light Press, 2009.)
Crazy Star (Loess Hills Books, 2005.)
Mental: Stories by Rock L'Orange (Publish America, 2005.)
Loving the Good Driver (Mellen Poetry Press, 1996, 2003.)
Islands (Conestoga Zen Press, 1999.)
Lord of the Apes (Conestoga Zen Press, 1997.)
Tiresias Strung-Out on a Half Can of Pepsi (Blue Light Press, 1993.)
Halves (Contemporary Review Press, 1988.)

Anthologies:

Collateral Damage (Ed. by Ami Kaye, et al., Glass Lyre Press, 2019.)
Carrying the Branch (Ed. by Ami Kaye, et al., Glass Lyre Press, 2017.)
Aeolian Harp, Volume One (Ed. by Ami Kaye, et al., Glass Lyre Press, 2016.)
River of Earth and Sky: Poems for the Twenty-First Century (Ed. by Diane Frank, Blue Light Press, 2014.)

Poetry at Round Top Anthology (Ed. by Jack Brannon, Round Top Festival Institute, 2012.)

This Enduring Gift (Ed. by Freddy Fonseca, 1st World, 2010.)

The Complete New Yorker (Ed. by New Yorker staff, Random House, 2005.)

The Dryland Fish (Ed. by Matthew MacLeod, 1st World, 2003.)

Eclipsed Moon Coins: Twenty-Six Visionary Poets (Ed. by Diane Frank, Blue Light Press, 1997.)

Voices on the Landscape: Contemporary Iowa Poets (Ed. by Michael Carey and Bob Neymeyer, Loess Hills Books, 1996.)

Forty Days and Forty Nights (Ed. by Bruce Williams, Iowa Arts Council, 1993.)

Collecting Moon Coins, Volume II (Ed. by Diane Frank, Blue Light Press, 1991.)

Lightning Source UK Ltd.
Milton Keynes UK
UKHW040931201020
371904UK00001B/86